Debi Goins-Francis is an accomplished author and retired attorney with a passion for inspiring others through her writing. She has previously penned three beloved children's books and now turns her focus to her latest project, a 21-day Christian devotional designed to enrich readers' spiritual journeys. When she's not writing, Debi enjoys exploring the world through reading and photography, always seeking new adventures and experiences to share. With a heart for faith and a commitment to helping others grow, Debi invites you to join her on this transformative journey.

This book is dedicated to all the remarkable individuals who have poured their love, wisdom, and guidance into my life. Their unwavering support and encouragement have shaped my journey and inspired me to share my faith with others.

Debra Goins-Francis

COME THIRSTY: LEAVE QUENCHED

AUSTIN MACAULEY PUBLISHERS

LONDON · CAMBRIDGE · NEW YORK · SHARJAH

Ordering Information
Quantity sales: Special discounts are available on quantity purchases by corporations, associations, and others. For details, contact the publisher at the address below.

Publisher's Cataloging-in-Publication data
Goins-Francis, Debra
Come Thirsty: Leave Quenched

ISBN 9798891556355 (Paperback)
ISBN 9798891556362 (Hardback)
ISBN 9798891556386 (ePub e-book)
ISBN 9798891556379 (Audiobook)

Library of Congress Control Number: 2024921172

www.austinmacauley.com/us

First Published 2025
Austin Macauley Publishers LLC
40 Wall Street, 33rd Floor, Suite 3302
New York, NY 10005
USA

mail-usa@austinmacauley.com
+1 (646) 5125767

🙏All glory and praise belong to God, and God alone who equips us and empowers us to do His work! 🙏

❧ prologue ❧

In the depths of our souls, we carry a thirst that cannot be quenched by the world. It is a thirst for meaning, purpose, and a deeper connection. However, when we come to the well of God's presence, with hearts open and thirsty, we find that His love and grace are an endless stream; satisfying our deepest longings and leaving us forever quenched and refreshed!!

In a world where the noise of daily life can easily drown out our deepest desires, this devotional serves as a location tracker – a navigational system pointing us towards the path of inner fulfillment. Each day I invite you to pause, reflect, and embrace the opportunity for spiritual nourishment. It is a reminder that no matter how arid your circumstances may seem, there is an oasis of inspiration and empowerment waiting for you.

Drawing from timeless wisdom traditions, the passages in "Come Thirsty, Leave Quenched" are akin to an invitation, an offer of solace, a gentle reminder. Whether you seek respite from a broken heart, a weary mind, or simply a place to ponder life's profound questions, this devotional is here to refresh your soul.

As you immerse yourself in these words, may you find the courage to confront your challenges, the strength to persevere, and the wisdom to truly drink from the wellspring of life.

So, dear reader, come. Come with a heart open to transformation, with a thirst unquenched, and leave these pages forever changed – awakened to a world of spiritual abundance beckoning you towards wholeness, harmony, and a life truly lived.

In John 4:14, Jesus spoke these words: "But whoever drinks the water I give them will never thirst. Indeed, the water I give them will become in them a spring of water welling up to eternal life." Let this journey be the catalyst that helps you realize the truth behind those words. You are ready. The time is now. Come……drink from the fountain that shall never run dry!

Welcome to your oasis.

Debi Goins-Francis

O

✔ Day 1: "Thirsting for God's Presence" (Revelation 22:17)

"The Spirit and the bride say, 'Come!' And let him who hears say, 'Come!' Let him who is thirsty come, and let everyone who wishes take the free gift of the water of life."

This invitation is extended to each one of us to come along on this expedition. We are invited to come to the most abundant water source, to approach God's presence, and to drink deeply from the water of life.

Dwelling deep in the recesses of our souls is a longing for something more, a yearning for meaning, a craving for purpose, and a hunger for a deeper connection to something. We often find ourselves searching for fulfillment in the things of this world, only to be left unsatisfied and thirsty.

But there is a reservoir, a source of living water, that can truly quench our thirst. It is the well of God's presence. When we come to this water source with open and thirsty hearts, we discover that His love and grace are an endless stream, flowing freely to satisfy our deepest longings.

When we come to the well, we find that God's love and grace are boundless. They overflow, filling us to the brim and beyond. We are refreshed, renewed, and forever changed. Our deepest longings are met, and our souls are satisfied.

So, dear reader, here we are as together we embark on this 21-day devotional journey. Let us come thirsty, with hearts open and ready to receive. Let us approach the well of God's presence, knowing that His love and grace will quench our thirst like nothing else can. May this devotional be a source of encouragement, inspiration, and transformation as we drink deeply from the well and leave forever quenched.

❧ A Deeper Dive ❧

Reflect on your thirst and the invitation to come to the well of God's presence. Take a moment to identify areas in your life where you have felt unsatisfied and thirsty, and commit to seeking fulfillment in God alone.

🫖 PEARLS OF WISDOM 🫖

Did you know?* Some wells are artesian, naturally pressurized, allowing water to flow without pumping. *Like the artesian well, God's love naturally flows into our lives when we open our hearts to Him.

☑ Day 2: "Living Water that Satisfies"

(John 6:35)

Today, we are invited to reflect on Jesus as the living water and to embrace the concept of flowing with the rhythm of God's grace. The focus on the metaphor of a stream encourages us to explore the concept of Jesus as the Living Water, a constant stream that fulfills the soul's deepest longing.

The key verse for this day is John 6:35, which says, "Then Jesus declared, 'I am the bread of life. Whoever comes to me will never go hungry, and whoever believes in me will never be thirsty.'"

In this verse, Jesus uses the metaphor of bread and water to illustrate the spiritual nourishment and satisfaction that He provides. He describes Himself as the bread of life, emphasizing that those who come to Him will never go hungry, and those who believe in Him will never be thirsty. This metaphor highlights the idea that Jesus is the ultimate source of fulfillment and satisfaction for our souls.

Just as bread and water are essential for physical sustenance, Jesus is essential for our spiritual sustenance. He is the living water that quenches our deepest thirst and satisfies our souls. He offers a constant stream of grace, love, and provision that never runs dry.

The concept of a stream implies movement and flow. It suggests that the grace and love of God are not stagnant or limited, but rather continuously flowing and available to us. As we embrace this concept, we are encouraged to flow with the rhythm of God's grace, allowing His love and provision to guide and sustain us.

To flow with the rhythm of God's grace means to align our lives with His will and to trust in His timing and direction. It involves surrendering our own desires and plans to His greater purpose and allowing His love to flow through us to others. It means seeking His guidance and wisdom in every aspect of our lives and relying on His strength and provision.

As we embrace Jesus as the living water and allow His grace to flow through us, we experience a deep sense of fulfillment and satisfaction. Our souls are nourished, and our deepest longings are met. We no longer need to search for fulfillment in the things of this world because we have found the ultimate source of satisfaction in Jesus.

May we come to Him with open hearts, ready to receive His love and provision, and may we allow His grace to guide and sustain us as we journey through life.

🥨A Deeper Dive.... 🥨

Dive deeper into Scripture and discover the promises of God that can quench your thirst. Choose one promise that resonates with you and meditate on that promise throughout the day.

🫖PEARLS OF WISDOM 🫖

Did you know? * Streams can vary in speed, influencing the surrounding ecosystem. *Our spiritual journey, like a stream, adapts and influences our inner ecosystem as we grow in faith.

🍇🍉🍉🍉🍉🍉

✅Day 3: "Thirsting for God's Guidance and Direction"

Today we are invited to reflect on seeking God in the vastness of our souls, finding stillness, and recognizing His presence as a source of peace and purpose.

(Psalm 143:6)

"I spread out my hands to you; I thirst for you like a parched land."

In this verse, the psalmist expresses a deep longing and thirst for God. They spread out their hands, a gesture of surrender and openness, as they seek to connect with God in the vastness of their soul. The metaphor of a parched land emphasizes their desperate need for God's presence and the satisfaction that only He can provide.

The image of a lake represents the vastness of our souls. Just as a lake is expansive and deep, our souls have a depth that can only be fully explored and understood by God. It is in this vastness that we are invited to seek God, to dive deep into the depths of our being and connect with Him.

When we seek God in the vastness of our souls, we find stillness. Just as a lake is calm and peaceful, our souls can find rest and tranquility in His presence. In the busyness and chaos of life, it is in the stillness of our souls that we can hear His voice and experience His peace.

Recognizing God's presence in the vastness of our souls also brings a sense of purpose. Just as a lake serves a purpose in providing water, sustaining life, and reflecting the beauty around it, our souls have a purpose in reflecting God's love and glory to the world. When we connect with God in the depths of our being, we discover our true identity and calling.

May we spread out our hands in surrender and thirst for Him like a parched land. May we also dive deep into the depths of our being and connect with Him, finding rest, peace, and a sense of purpose in His presence.

❀A Deeper Dive…. ❀

What are the distractions that keep you from drinking deeply from the well of God's presence? Identify one distraction and take a practical step to minimize its influence on your life.

PEARLS OF WISDOM

Did you know? * Lakes have distinct layers, each supporting different forms of life.

- *Parallel: * Our souls, like the layers of a lake, harbor different aspects waiting to be discovered in God's presence.

✔ Day 4: "Hungering and Thirsting for Righteousness"

Today we are invited to reflect on the metaphor of a river and the concept of purity of heart as we navigate through life's journey with God.

(Matthew 5:6)

"Blessed are those who hunger and thirst for righteousness, for they will be filled."

In this verse, Jesus speaks to His disciples about the importance of hungering and thirsting for righteousness. The metaphor of a river represents the purity of heart that comes from seeking after God and His righteousness.

A river is a flowing body of water that is constantly moving and changing. It is often associated with life, refreshment, and sustenance. Similarly, the purity of heart that comes from hungering and thirsting for righteousness is a dynamic and transformative process.

Hungering and thirsting for righteousness means desiring to live in alignment with God's will and His standards of righteousness. It involves seeking after God's truth, His ways, and His character. It is a deep longing to be filled with His righteousness and to live a life that reflects His goodness and love.

Just as a river brings life and sustenance to the land it flows through, the purity of heart that comes from hungering and thirsting for righteousness brings spiritual life and nourishment to our souls. It enables us to experience the fullness of God's presence and to walk in His ways.

The journey of hungering and thirsting for righteousness is not always easy. It requires a willingness to let go of our own desires and to submit to God's will. It involves seeking after Him with our whole heart, mind, and soul. It is a continuous process of surrendering to His leading and allowing Him to purify our hearts.

May we hunger and thirst for righteousness, seeking after God and His ways. May we allow His presence and His truth to flow through our lives, bringing refreshment, life, and transformation. And may we be filled with His righteousness, experiencing the blessings and fulfillment that come from walking in His ways.

🐝A Deeper Dive.... 🐝

Cultivate a daily habit of seeking God's presence through prayer. Set aside a specific time each day to connect with Him and commit to this daily practice.

🐣PEARLS OF WISDOM 🐣

Did you know? * Rivers can meander and create intricate patterns over time.

— *Parallel: * Our life journey with God may have twists and turns, shaping us into unique individuals.

✅Day 5: "A Well-Watered Garden"

(Isaiah 58:11)

Today we will focus on the metaphor of a spring and explore the concept of God's guidance springing forth to provide renewal and direction in moments of spiritual thirst.

The key verse for this day is Isaiah 58:11, which says, "The Lord will guide you always; he will satisfy your needs in a sun-scorched land and will strengthen your frame. You will be like a well-watered garden, like a spring whose waters never fail."

In this verse, Isaiah speaks of the Lord's guidance and provision in times of spiritual thirst. The metaphor of spring represents the refreshing and life-giving water that God provides to quench our spiritual thirst. Just as spring flows with constant and abundant water, God's guidance and provision are always available to us.

God's guidance springs forth to provide renewal and direction in moments of spiritual thirst. When we feel spiritually dry and in need of direction, God's guidance is like a refreshing spring that revives and rejuvenates our souls. His guidance leads us on the right path and provides the nourishment and sustenance we need to thrive.

In a sun-scorched land, where the heat is intense and the ground is dry, a spring brings relief and renewal. Similarly, in the challenges and trials of life, when our souls feel parched and weary, God's guidance and provision bring refreshment and strength. He satisfies our needs and strengthens us, enabling us to persevere and overcome.

When we embrace God's guidance and provision, our lives become like well-watered gardens. A well-watered garden is lush, vibrant, and fruitful. It represents a life that is flourishing and abundant. As we allow God's guidance to spring forth in our lives, we experience spiritual growth, bear fruit, and become a source of blessing to others.

We are invited to reflect on the metaphor of spring and the concept of God's guidance springing forth to provide renewal and direction in moments of spiritual thirst. May we open our hearts to receive His guidance and provision, allowing His refreshing waters to quench our spiritual thirst and lead us on the path of renewal and abundance.

❧A Deeper Dive.... ❧

Reflect on the ways in which you have settled for temporary satisfaction instead of seeking the eternal satisfaction found in God. Identify one area where you have been settling and take a step towards seeking true fulfillment.

PEARLS OF WISDOM

Did you know?* Some springs emerge from caves, symbolizing hidden sources.
   – *Parallel:* God's guidance, like a spring, comes from hidden depths, revealing His wisdom in our lives.

✓ Day 6: "Living Water"

(John 7:37)

Our focus today is on the metaphor of a pond and we are invited to contemplate Jesus as the living water, offering us peace and tranquility while satisfying the soul's deep thirst.

The key verse for this day is John 7:37, which says, "On the last and greatest day of the festival, Jesus stood and said in a loud voice, 'Let anyone who is thirsty come to me and drink.'"

In this verse, Jesus lovingly extends the invitation to all who are thirsty to come to Him and drink. He presents Himself as the source of living water, the one who can satisfy the deepest longings of our souls. The metaphor of a pond represents the tranquility and peacefulness that Jesus offers when we come to Him and drink from the wellspring of His love and grace.

Just as a pond provides a calm and serene environment, Jesus offers us peace and tranquility in the midst of life's storms. When we come to Him with our thirst, our burdens, and our anxieties, He provides a sense of calm and rest for our souls. He is the one who can quiet the storms within us and bring a deep sense of peace.

Drinking from the living water that Jesus offers also satisfies the deep thirst of our souls. The world offers temporary satisfaction, but Jesus offers eternal fulfillment. When we come to Him and drink, our souls are nourished and satisfied. We no longer need to search for fulfillment in the things of this world because we have found the ultimate source of satisfaction in Jesus.

On Day 6 of this devotional journey, we are invited to consider Jesus as the living water, offering tranquility and satisfying the soul's deep thirst. May we come to Him with open hearts, ready to receive His peace and fulfillment. May we drink deeply from the wellspring of His love and grace, finding rest and satisfaction for our souls.

&A Deeper Dive…. &

Explore the concept of surrender and how it relates to quenching your spiritual thirst. Surrender one area of your life to God and trust Him to provide the satisfaction you long for.

☙PEARLS OF WISDOM ☙

Did you know?* Ponds provide habitat diversity, supporting various life forms.

– *Parallel:* God's presence in the quiet moments, like a pond, sustains and nurtures the diversity within our souls.

✓Day 7: "God's Abundant Provision"

(Psalm 107:9)

Today we focus on the metaphor of a fountain as we explore the concept of God's satisfying and refreshing grace, highlighting His abundant provision.

The key verse for this day is Psalm 107:9, which says, "For he satisfies the thirsty and fills the hungry with good things."

In this verse, the psalmist declares that God satisfies the thirsty and fills the hungry with good things. The metaphor of a fountain represents the abundant and overflowing grace of God. Just as a fountain continuously pours out water, God's grace is constantly available to quench our spiritual thirst and provide for our needs.

God's grace is satisfying and refreshing. When we come to Him with a thirsty soul, He pours out His grace upon us, filling us with His love, mercy, and forgiveness. His grace satisfies the deepest longings of our hearts and brings a sense of fulfillment and contentment. It is through His grace that we find true satisfaction and joy.

God's grace is also abundant. Just as a fountain overflows with water, God's grace overflows in our lives. He provides more than enough for our needs and blesses us abundantly. His grace is not limited or scarce, but rather limitless and abundant. We can trust that He will always provide for us and meet our every need.

As we experience God's satisfying and refreshing grace, we are called to share it with others. Just as a fountain spreads water to nourish the surrounding area, we are called to spread God's grace to those around us. We are called to be channels of His grace, extending love, mercy, and forgiveness to others. Through our words and actions, we can reflect the abundant provision of God's grace to a world in need.

As we continue our trek through this devotional journey, we are invited to delve into the concept of God's satisfying and refreshing grace, highlighting His abundant provision. May we come to Him with thirsty souls, ready to receive His grace and find true satisfaction. May we also be channels of His grace, spreading His love and mercy to those around us.

🐝 A Deeper Dive.... 🐝

Reflect on the transformative power of encountering God's love and grace. Consider how encountering His presence has changed your perspective, purpose, and fulfillment. Share your testimony with someone today.

🐚PEARLS OF WISDOM 🐚

Did you know? * Fountains can be designed to reach different heights and patterns.

- *Parallel: * God's grace, like a fountain, is diverse and reaches us in unique ways, shaping our spiritual experience.

✅ Day 8: God's Overflowing Grace

(Matthew 6:33)

Today our focus is on the metaphor of a waterfall and we are encouraged to seek God's kingdom as the ultimate source of satisfaction and blessings.

The key verse for this day is Matthew 6:33, which says, "But seek first his kingdom and his righteousness, and all these things will be given to you as well."

In this verse, Jesus teaches the importance of seeking God's kingdom above all else. He assures us that when we prioritize seeking God and His righteousness, He will provide for our needs and bless us abundantly. The metaphor of a waterfall represents the cascade of transformative blessings that flow into our lives when we seek God's kingdom.

A waterfall is a powerful and awe-inspiring sight. It represents abundance, strength, and beauty. Similarly, when we seek God's kingdom, we tap into the abundant blessings and transformative power that flow from Him. His blessings cascade into our lives, bringing transformation, provision, and fulfillment.

Seeking God's kingdom involves aligning our hearts and priorities with His will. It means seeking His righteousness, living in obedience to His commands, and pursuing a relationship with Him above all else. When we prioritize seeking God and His kingdom, we experience a deep sense of satisfaction and fulfillment that cannot be found in the things of this world.

As we seek God's kingdom, He provides for our needs. Just as a waterfall provides water for the surrounding area, God provides for our physical, emotional, and spiritual needs. He knows what we need even before we ask, and He is faithful to provide. When we seek Him first, we can trust that He will take care of us and meet our every need.

As we plunge deeper into this devotional journey, we are encouraged to seek God's kingdom as the ultimate source of satisfaction and blessings. May we prioritize seeking God above all else, aligning our hearts and priorities with His will. As we seek Him, may we experience the cascade of life-altering blessings that flow from His abundant grace. May we trust that He will provide for our needs and bless us abundantly as we seek Him first.

❧A Deeper Dive.... ❧

Embrace the truth that you are a vessel of God's love and grace. Identify one person in your life who needs to experience His love and commit to showing them kindness and compassion.

☝PEARLS OF WISDOM ☝

Did you know? * Some waterfalls freeze partially in winter, creating stunning ice formations.

- *Parallel: * God's transformative power, like a frozen waterfall, can create beauty even in challenging seasons of our lives.

☑ Day 9: "Finding Spiritual Refreshment"

(Isaiah 44:3)

Today we focus on the metaphor of a creek as we explore the concept of God pouring His Spirit into the thirsty soul, meandering through the landscape of life.

The key verse for this day is Isaiah 44:3, which says, "For I will pour water on the thirsty land, and streams on the dry ground; I will pour out my Spirit on your offspring, and my blessing on your descendants."

In this verse, God promises to pour out His Spirit on the thirsty land and bless the descendants of His people. The metaphor of a creek represents the flowing and meandering movement of God's Spirit in the lives of believers. Just as a creek brings life and nourishment to the land it passes through, God's Spirit brings spiritual life and refreshment to the thirsty soul.

When our souls are thirsty for God, He pours out His Spirit upon us. His Spirit brings renewal, restoration, and spiritual growth. It satisfies our deepest longings and quenches our spiritual thirst. The presence of God's Spirit in our lives brings a sense of peace, joy, and fulfillment that cannot be found in the things of this world.

The meandering movement of a creek represents the journey of life. As God's Spirit meanders through the landscape of our lives, it guides, directs, and empowers us. His Spirit leads us on the path of righteousness, helps us navigate through challenges and obstacles, and enables us to bear fruit in our lives.

God's Spirit also brings blessings to our offspring. When we have a relationship with God and His Spirit dwells within us, His blessings extend to future generations. Our children, their children and their children's children can experience the transforming power of God's Spirit and receive His blessings as well.

As we surf through this devotional journey, we are invited to explore the metaphor of a creek and the concept of God pouring His Spirit into the thirsty soul, meandering through the landscape of life. May we open our hearts to receive the outpouring of God's Spirit, allowing His presence to bring spiritual life, refreshment, and guidance. May we also recognize the impact of God's Spirit on future generations, as His blessings extend to our descendants.

🐝 A Deeper Dive…. 🐝

Reflect on the importance of community in quenching your spiritual thirst. Reach out to someone in your church or community and offer your support and encouragement.

🍊 PEARLS OF WISDOM 🍊

Creek: **
*Did you know? * Creeks often form meanders, showcasing the dynamic nature of water.

- *Parallel: * God's Spirit, like a meandering creek, guides us dynamically through the changing landscapes of life.

✅ Day 10: "The Reservoir of Life"

(John 14:6)

Our focus today is on the metaphor of a reservoir and explores the concept of Jesus as the way, the truth, and the life.

The key verse is John 14:6, which says, "Jesus answered, 'I am the way and the truth and the life. No one comes to the Father except through me.'"

In this verse, Jesus declares Himself as the way, the truth, and the life. The metaphor of a reservoir represents Jesus as a source of divine guidance and nourishment for our spiritual thirst. Just as a reservoir holds a vast amount of water, Jesus holds the wisdom, truth, and life-giving power that we need to navigate our spiritual journey.

Jesus is the way. He is the path that leads us to the Father. Through His life, death, and resurrection, He has made a way for us to have a relationship with God. He is the ultimate guide who shows us the way to eternal life and leads us on the path of righteousness. When we follow Jesus, we are on the right path, walking in alignment with God's will.

Jesus is the truth. In a world filled with deception and falsehood, Jesus is the embodiment of truth. He reveals to us the true nature of God, the reality of our sin, and the way to salvation. His teachings and His life reflect the truth of God's love, grace, and redemption. When we seek truth, we find it in Jesus.

Jesus is the life. He is the source of abundant and eternal life. Through His sacrifice, He offers us forgiveness, reconciliation with God, and the promise of eternal life. When we have a relationship with Jesus, we experience true life – a life filled with purpose, joy, and fulfillment. He quenches our spiritual thirst and satisfies the deepest longings of our souls.

As we journey on, we are invited to reflect on the metaphor of a reservoir and the concept of Jesus as the way, the truth, and the life. May we recognize Jesus as the ultimate source of divine guidance and nourishment for our spiritual thirst. May we follow Him as our guide, seek truth in His teachings, and experience the abundant life that He offers.

🐝 A Deeper Dive…. 🐝

Dive deeper into worship and praise as a way to connect with God's presence. Set aside time today to worship Him through music, prayer, or creative expression.

🐚PEARLS OF WISDOM 🐚

Reservoir: **

- *Did you know? * Reservoirs are vital for regulating water supply and preventing floods.
- *Parallel: * God's guidance, like a reservoir, helps regulate the flow of our lives, preventing overwhelming challenges.

✅ Day 11: "Diving into God's Overflow"

(Psalm 36:8)

Today we focus on the metaphor of a rain barrel and invites us to reflect on God's abundance overflowing, even in the small blessings of life.

The key verse is Psalm 36:8, which says, "They feast on the abundance of your house; you give them drink from your river of delights."

In this verse, the psalmist acknowledges that God's house is filled with abundance. The metaphor of a rain barrel represents the overflowing abundance of God's blessings in our lives, even in the seemingly small and insignificant things. Just as a rain barrel collects and stores water, God's abundance fills every aspect of our lives.

God's abundance is not limited to material possessions or grand gestures. It extends to the everyday blessings that we often overlook. It is in the small moments of joy, the provision of our basic needs, and the beauty of creation that we can see God's abundant blessings. He provides for us in ways that we may not always recognize, but His provision is constant and overflowing.

When we feast on the abundance of God's house, we recognize and appreciate the blessings He pours into our lives. We find satisfaction and contentment in His provision, knowing that He is faithful to meet our needs. We drink from His river of delights, experiencing the joy and fulfillment that come from being in a relationship with Him.

As we reflect on the metaphor of a rain barrel, we are reminded to be grateful for the small blessings in life. We are encouraged to cultivate an attitude of gratitude and to recognize God's constant provision, even in seemingly insignificant things. When we have eyes to see and a heart of gratitude, we can truly feast on the abundance of God's house and drink from His river of delights.

An invitation has been extended to us to reflect on the metaphor of a rain barrel and the concept of God's abundance overflowing, even in the small blessings of life. May we open our hearts to recognize and appreciate the everyday blessings that God pours into our lives. May we feast on His abundance and drink from His river of delights, finding joy and contentment in His constant provision.

❧ A Deeper Dive.... ❧

Explore the concept of gratitude and how it can quench your spiritual thirst. Take a moment to write down three things you are grateful for and express your gratitude to God.

🫖 PEARLS OF WISDOM 🫖

Rain Barrel: **
- — *Did you know? * Rain barrels conserve water, promoting sustainability.
- — *Parallel: * Our gratitude for God's blessings, like a rain barrel, promotes spiritual sustainability and mindful living.

✅ Day 12: "Rest and Renewal"

(John 6:35)

Today our focus is on the metaphor of an oasis which encourages us to find refuge in Christ, a sanctuary in the desert of life's challenges.

The key verse is John 6:35, which says, "Then Jesus declared, 'I am the bread of life. Whoever comes to me will never go hungry, and whoever believes in me will never be thirsty.'"

In this verse, Jesus declares Himself as the bread of life. The metaphor of an oasis represents Christ as a source of refreshment, nourishment, and shelter in the midst of life's challenges. Just as an oasis provides relief and sustenance in the desert, Jesus offers us refuge and sustenance for our souls.

Life can often feel like a desert, filled with adversities, hardships, and extreme dryness. In the midst of these difficulties, Jesus invites us to come to Him and find refuge. He is the oasis in the desert, offering us rest, comfort, and renewal. When we come to Him, we find solace for our weary souls and strength to face the challenges of life.

Just as an oasis provides water to quench our physical thirst, Jesus satisfies our spiritual thirst. He offers us living water that springs up to eternal life. When we believe in Him and have a relationship with Him, our spiritual thirst is quenched, and we find true satisfaction and fulfillment in Him.

In addition to providing refreshment and nourishment, an oasis also offers shelter and protection from the harsh elements of the desert. Similarly, Jesus is our sanctuary in the midst of life's challenges. He is our refuge, our safe haven, and our source of strength. In Him, we find comfort, peace, and security, knowing that He is with us and will never leave us.

We are invited to explore the metaphor of an oasis and the concept of finding refuge in Christ, a sanctuary in the desert of life's challenges. May we come to Jesus, the bread of life, and find refreshment, nourishment, and shelter in Him. May we drink from the living water He offers and find satisfaction for our souls. May we take refuge in Him, knowing that He is our safe haven and source of strength in the midst of life's challenges.

ᴥA **Deeper Dive....** ᴥ

Reflect on the power of forgiveness in finding true satisfaction. Identify someone you need to forgive and take a step towards reconciliation and healing.

PEARLS OF WISDOM

Oasis: **
- — *Did you know? * Oases are biodiversity hotspots in deserts, supporting various life forms.
- — *Parallel: * God's presence, like an oasis, brings life and abundance even in the dry seasons of our spiritual journey.

✓ Day 13: "God's Healing Touch"

(Psalm 23:2)

We focus today on the metaphor of a hot spring and explore the concept of God's comforting presence as a source of healing and restoration.

The key verse is Psalm 23:2, which says, "He makes me lie down in green pastures, he leads me beside quiet waters."

In this verse, the psalmist describes God as a shepherd who provides rest and refreshment for His sheep. The metaphor of a hot spring represents God's comforting presence, akin to a soothing and healing source of water. Just as a hot spring offers relaxation and healing to those who immerse themselves in its waters, God's presence brings comfort and restoration to our weary souls.

A hot spring is known for its therapeutic properties. The warm water can soothe tired muscles, relieve stress, and promote relaxation. Similarly, God's comforting presence brings healing and restoration to our souls. When we come into His presence, we find solace and peace. He calms our anxieties, eases our burdens, and brings comfort to our weary hearts.

Just as a hot spring is a place of tranquility and serenity, God's presence offers a refuge from the chaos and busyness of life. In His presence, we can find rest and restoration. He leads us beside quiet waters, where we can experience a deep sense of peace and rejuvenation.

God's comforting presence also brings healing to our wounded hearts and broken spirits. Just as the warm waters of a hot spring can soothe physical ailments, God's presence can heal our emotional and spiritual wounds. He is the ultimate source of healing and restoration, offering comfort, hope, and renewal to those who seek Him.

Today we are invited to delve into the metaphor of a hot spring and the concept of God's comforting presence as a source of healing and restoration.

May we find solace and peace in His presence, experiencing the soothing and healing power of His love. May we allow His comforting presence to bring rest and rejuvenation to our weary souls. May we open our hearts to His healing touch, allowing Him to bring healing and restoration to our wounded hearts and broken spirits.

❧A **Deeper Dive....** ❧

Plunge deeper into God's Word and discover His promises for your life. Choose one promise that speaks to your current situation and meditate on it throughout the day.

🫗PEARLS OF WISDOM 🫗

Hot Spring (Psalm 23:2):**
- — *Did you know? * Hot springs are known for therapeutic benefits, soothing both body and mind.
- — *Parallel: * God's comforting presence, like a hot spring, brings healing and peace to our souls.

✅Day 14: "Growing in Grace"

(Isaiah 55:1)

Today we focus on the metaphor of a glacier and invites us to reflect on God's patience in the slow but transformative journey of our lives.

The key verse is Isaiah 55:1, which says, "Come, all you who are thirsty, come to the waters; and you who have no money, come, buy and eat! Come, buy wine and milk without money and without cost."

In this verse, God extends an invitation to those who are thirsty and in need. The metaphor of a glacier represents the slow and gradual process of transformation that takes place in our lives. Just as a glacier moves slowly but has the power to shape and transform the landscape, God's transformative power works in our lives over time, bringing about deep and lasting change.

God's patience is evident in His invitation to come and receive without cost. He offers us the opportunity to buy and eat, to partake in the abundance of His provision, even when we have nothing to offer in return. His transformative power is not dependent on our own efforts or resources but on His grace and love.

The journey of transformation can be slow and challenging. It requires patience, perseverance, and trust in God's timing. Just as a glacier takes time to carve out valleys and shape the land, God's transformative work in our lives unfolds gradually. He works in the depths of our hearts, shaping us into the image of Christ and molding us into vessels of His love and grace.

The depth of God's transformative power is beyond our comprehension. Just as a glacier's impact on the landscape is vast and far-reaching, God's transformative work in our lives has a profound and lasting effect. He has the power to change our hearts, renew our minds, and transform our lives from the inside out.

The invitation is extended today to reflect on the metaphor of a glacier and the concept of God's patience in the slow but transformative journey of our lives.

May we embrace the process of transformation, trusting in God's timing and relying on His grace. May we recognize the depth of His transformative power and allow Him to shape us into vessels of His love and grace. May we come to Him, thirsty and in need, and receive His abundant provision without cost.

ᥐA **Deeper Dive....** ᥐ

Reflect on the ways in which you have been seeking fulfillment in worldly pursuits. Identify one area where you have been seeking satisfaction outside of God and commit to redirecting your focus.

ᥤPEARLS OF WISDOM ᥤ

Glacier (Isaiah 55:1 – Again): **
- — *Did you know? * Glaciers store ancient information about the Earth's climate in their ice layers.
- — *Parallel: * God's patient work in our lives, like a glacier, holds the depth of ancient wisdom that shapes our spiritual journey.

✔**Day 15: "Unfathomable Love"**

(Revelation 21:6)

Today our focus is on the metaphor of an iceberg which invites us to reflect on God's vastness and depth, which may be unseen but are powerful and offer a perspective on the magnitude of His love.

The key verse is Revelation 21:6, which says, "He said to me: 'It is done. I am the Alpha and the Omega, the Beginning and the End. To the thirsty, I will give water without cost from the spring of the water of life.'"

In this verse, God declares Himself as the Alpha and the Omega, the Beginning and the End. The metaphor of an iceberg represents the vastness and depth of God, which may be unseen but are powerful and awe-inspiring. Just as an iceberg extends deep beneath the surface of the water, God's love and power extend far beyond what we can see or comprehend.

An iceberg is a massive structure, with only a small portion visible above the water. Similarly, God's vastness and depth are beyond our human understanding. His love, wisdom, and power are immeasurable and extend far beyond our limited perspective. We can only catch a glimpse of His greatness, but even that glimpse is enough to leave us in awe.

The unseen portion of an iceberg is often the most powerful. It is the part that can cause ships to sink and shape the landscape. Similarly, the unseen aspects of God's character and work in our lives are often the most transformative and impactful. His love, grace, and power work in ways that we may not always understand or perceive, but their effects are profound and life-changing.

God's love is vast and all-encompassing. It is deeper than we can fathom and wider than we can imagine. His love knows no bounds and extends to every corner of creation. When we are thirsty and in need, He offers us the water of life without cost. His love is freely given, and it satisfies the deepest longings of our souls.

On Day 15 of this devotional journey, we are invited to reflect on the metaphor of an iceberg and the concept of God's vastness and depth, which may be unseen but are powerful and offer a perspective on the magnitude of His love. May we stand in awe of God's greatness, recognizing that His love and power extend far beyond what we can see or comprehend. May we embrace the transformative and life-changing work of His love in our lives. And may we come to Him, thirsty and in need, and receive the water of life that He freely offers.

❧A **Deeper Dive....** ❧

Cultivate a spirit of generosity and giving as a way to quench your spiritual thirst. Identify one way you can bless someone today and take action on it.

🍊PEARLS OF WISDOM 🍊

Iceberg (Revelation 21:6): **
- *Did you know? * Only a small portion of an iceberg is visible above the waterline.
- *Parallel: * God's vastness, like an iceberg, has unseen depths that impact our lives in profound ways.

✅ Day 16: "Thirsting Hearts"

(Psalm 42:1-2)

Today we focus on the metaphor of a watering hole and are encouraged to cultivate a communal thirst for God's presence.

The key verses are taken from Psalm 42:1-2, which says, "As the deer pants for streams of water, so my soul pants for you, my God. My soul thirsts for God, for the living God. When can I go and meet with God?"

In these verses, the psalmist expresses a deep longing and thirst for God's presence. The metaphor of a watering hole represents a place where animals gather to drink and satisfy their thirst. Similarly, the psalmist longs for a place where they can meet with God and find refreshment for their soul.

The psalmist's desire for God's presence is not an individual longing but a communal one. They use the imagery of a deer panting for streams of water to illustrate the intensity of their thirst for God. This imagery highlights the shared experience of longing and seeking God's presence together.

Just as animals gather at a watering hole to quench their thirst, we are called to gather together as a community of believers to seek God's presence. When we come together in worship, prayer, and fellowship, our collective thirst for God's presence is magnified. We encourage and support one another in our pursuit of God, creating an atmosphere where His presence can be experienced more deeply.

The communal thirst for God's presence is a powerful force that unites believers and strengthens their faith. When we gather together with a shared longing for God, we create a space where His Spirit can move and work among us. We encourage one another, spur one another on in our faith, and experience the transformative power of God's presence together.

On Day 16 of this devotional journey, we are invited to reflect on the metaphor of a watering hole and the concept of cultivating a communal thirst for God's presence. May we long for God's presence in our own lives and also encourage and support one another in our pursuit of Him. May we gather together as a community of believers, thirsting for God's presence, and creating a space where His Spirit can move and work among us. And may we experience the transformative power of God's presence as we seek Him together.

❦ A **Deeper Dive**.... ❦

Reflect on the importance of rest and Sabbath in finding true satisfaction. Set aside time today to rest and rejuvenate, allowing God to fill you with His peace and joy.

PEARLS OF WISDOM

Watering Hole (Psalm 42:1-2):**
- — *Did you know? * Watering holes in nature serve as communal gathering points for various species.
- — *Parallel: * Our communal thirst for God's presence, like a watering hole, unites us in shared spiritual experiences.

✔ Day 17: Higher Ground

(Matthew 5:6)

Today we focus on the metaphor of a water tower which invites us to reflect on the elevated and steadfast pursuit of righteousness. The key verse for this day is Matthew 5:6, which says, "Blessed are those who hunger and thirst for righteousness, for they will be filled."

In this verse, Jesus teaches that those who hunger and thirst for righteousness will be blessed and filled. The metaphor of a water tower represents the elevated and steadfast pursuit of righteousness, emphasizing the hunger and thirst for God's ways.

A water tower is a tall structure that stores and provides a supply of water to a community. It stands high above the ground, symbolizing the elevated nature of righteousness. Similarly, the pursuit of righteousness requires us to elevate our thoughts, actions and desires to align with God's ways.

Hunger and thirst are powerful and intense desires. When we hunger and thirst for righteousness, we have a deep longing and craving to live in accordance with God's will. It is a hunger and thirst that cannot be satisfied by anything else but a close relationship with God and a life lived in obedience to His commands.

The pursuit of righteousness is not a one-time event but a steadfast and ongoing journey. It requires a daily commitment to seek God's ways, to align our thoughts and actions with His truth, and to live in obedience to His commands. It is a pursuit that requires discipline, perseverance, and a hunger and thirst for God's ways.

When we hunger and thirst for righteousness, we position ourselves to receive the blessings and fulfillment that come from living in alignment with God's will. We experience the satisfaction and contentment that can only be found in a close relationship with Him. Our lives become a testimony of His goodness and grace as we reflect His righteousness to the world around us.

On Day 17 of this devotional journey, we are invited to reflect on the metaphor of a water tower and the concept of the elevated and steadfast pursuit of righteousness. May we hunger and thirst for God's ways, seeking to align our thoughts, actions, and desires with His truth. May we commit to a daily pursuit of righteousness, knowing that in doing so, we will be blessed and filled. May our lives reflect His righteousness, becoming a testimony of His goodness and grace to the world around us.

❧ A **Deeper Dive....** ❧

Explore the concept of surrendering your plans and desires to God's will. Identify one area where you need to surrender control and trust God's perfect plan for your life.

PEARLS OF WISDOM

Water Tower (Matthew 5:6):**
- *Did you know?* Water towers maintain water pressure, ensuring a steady supply to communities.
- *Parallel:* Our hunger and thirst for righteousness, like a water tower, uphold the spiritual pressure that sustains and nourishes our souls.

✅ Day 18: "The Soul Restorer"

(Matthew 11:28)

Our focus today is on the metaphor of an artificial lake and invites us to reflect on finding rest in the collaborative efforts of humanity and God.

The key verse is Matthew 11:28, which says, "Come to me, all you who are weary and burdened, and I will give you rest."

In this verse, Jesus extends an invitation to those who are weary and burdened to come to Him and find rest. The metaphor of an artificial lake represents the collaborative efforts of humanity and God in creating a place of rest and beauty. It highlights the beauty and significance of shared responsibilities in finding rest.

An artificial lake is created through the collaborative efforts of engineers, laborers, and various stakeholders. It requires careful planning, hard work, and the coordination of different skills and resources. Similarly, finding rest in our lives often involves a collaborative effort between ourselves and God.

We are invited to come to Jesus and find rest, but this invitation requires our active participation. It involves surrendering our burdens, worries, and striving to Him and allowing Him to work in and through us. It requires us to trust in His guidance, rely on His strength, and cooperate with His transformative work in our lives.

Finding rest in the collaborative efforts of humanity and God also involves recognizing the beauty and significance of shared responsibilities. We are not meant to carry our burdens alone but to share them with God and with others. We are called to support and encourage one another, to bear one another's burdens, and to work together to create spaces of rest and beauty in our lives and in the world.

The collaborative efforts of humanity and God in finding rest also reflect the interconnectedness of our lives. Just as an artificial lake impacts the surrounding environment and ecosystems, our pursuit of rest and restoration can have a ripple effect on those around us. When we find rest in God, it not only benefits us but also has the potential to inspire and encourage others to seek rest in Him.

Today we are invited to reflect on the metaphor of an artificial lake and the concept of finding rest in the collaborative efforts of humanity and God.

May we come to Jesus, surrendering our burdens and finding rest in Him. May we recognize the beauty and significance of shared responsibilities in finding rest and supporting one another. And may our pursuit of rest have a ripple effect, inspiring others to seek rest in God as well.

⸙A Deeper Dive.... ⸙

Reflect on the ways in which you have been seeking validation and approval from others. Commit to finding your worth and identity in God alone.

PEARLS OF WISDOM

Artificial Lake (Matthew 11:28 – Again): **

-   *Did you know? * Artificial lakes can be designed to enhance beauty and recreation.
-   *Parallel: * Collaborative efforts with God, like an artificial lake, can create beauty and joy in our spiritual journeys.

✓Day 19: "The Power Within"

(Isaiah 55:1)

Today we focus on the metaphor of an aquifer and invites us to explore God's hidden strength within us, a deep well of resilience that sustains the soul.

The key verse is Isaiah 55:1, which says, "Come, all you who are thirsty, come to the waters; and you who have no money, come, buy and eat! Come, buy wine and milk without money and without cost."

In this verse, God extends an invitation to those who are thirsty and in need to come to Him and find sustenance. The metaphor of an aquifer represents the hidden strength and resilience that God has placed within us, like a deep well of water that sustains and nourishes the soul.

An aquifer is an underground layer of water-bearing rock or sediment that can be tapped into to provide a reliable source of water. It is a hidden reservoir that holds the life-giving resource of water, even in times of drought or scarcity. Similarly, God has placed within us a hidden strength and resilience that can sustain us in the midst of challenges and difficulties.

This hidden strength within us is not dependent on external circumstances or resources. It is a gift from God that is freely available to all who come to Him. Just as water from an aquifer is accessible to anyone who taps into it, God's strength and resilience are accessible to all who seek Him.

The deep well of resilience that God has placed within us enables us to endure and overcome the trials and hardships of life. It is a source of inner strength that sustains us when we feel weak or weary. It empowers us to keep going, to persevere, and to find hope and joy even in the midst of difficult circumstances.

God's hidden strength within us also reminds us that we are not alone in our struggles. He is with us, providing the sustenance and support we need. When we tap into His strength, we can find comfort, peace, and the ability to navigate life's challenges with resilience and grace.

The invitation is being extended to reflect on the metaphor of an aquifer and the concept of God's hidden strength within us.

May we come to Him, recognizing our thirst and need for His sustenance. May we tap into the deep well of resilience that He has placed within us, finding strength to endure and overcome. May we find comfort and support in His presence, knowing that He is with us in every season of life.

❧A Deeper Dive.... ❧

Dive deeper into prayer and intercession for others. Choose one person or situation to pray for fervently today and commit to praying consistently for them.

✤PEARLS OF WISDOM ✤

Aquifer (Isaiah 55:1 – Again): **
- *Did you know? * Aquifers hold vast amounts of water beneath the Earth's surface.
- *Parallel: * God's hidden strength within us, like an aquifer, is a deep well of resilience sustaining our spiritual lives.

✔️Day 20: "Living Waters"

(John 4:14)

Today we focus on the metaphor of a coastal lagoon and we are being beckoned to reflect on Jesus offering eternal life, which serves as a meeting point of salvation and fulfillment.

The key verse is John 4:14, which says, "But whoever drinks the water I give them will never thirst. Indeed, the water I give them will become in them a spring of water welling up to eternal life."

In this verse, Jesus speaks to the Samaritan woman at the well, offering her living water that will quench her spiritual thirst and lead to eternal life. The metaphor of a coastal lagoon represents the meeting point of salvation and fulfillment that Jesus offers through His gift of eternal life.

A coastal lagoon is a body of water that is connected to the ocean but separated by a barrier, such as a sandbar or a coral reef. It is a place where the freshwater from rivers and streams meets the saltwater of the ocean, creating a unique and diverse ecosystem. Similarly, Jesus offers us a meeting point where our spiritual thirst is quenched and our deepest longings are fulfilled.

The water that Jesus offers is not temporary or fleeting. It is living water that satisfies our spiritual thirst and brings us into a relationship with Him. It is a source of eternal life, a life that is abundant and full, both now and for all eternity.

Drinking the water that Jesus gives us signifies receiving His salvation and entering into a new life in Him. It is a transformative experience that brings about a deep sense of fulfillment and purpose. Just as a coastal lagoon is a place of beauty and abundance, the gift of eternal life in Jesus is a source of joy, peace, and fulfillment that surpasses anything the world can offer.

The meeting point of salvation and fulfillment in Jesus is not limited to a specific location or time. It is accessible to all who come to Him in faith, regardless of their background or circumstances. Jesus offers this gift freely to anyone who believes in Him and receives Him as their Lord and Savior.

On Day 20 of this devotional journey, we are invited to reflect on the metaphor of a coastal lagoon and the concept of Jesus offering eternal life as a meeting point of salvation and fulfillment. May we drink from the living water that He offers, allowing it to quench our spiritual thirst and bring us into a deep and fulfilling relationship with Him. May we experience the abundant life that comes from knowing Him and receiving His gift of eternal life. And may we find joy, peace, and fulfillment in the meeting point of salvation and fulfillment that Jesus provides.

❧A Deeper Dive.... ❧

Reflect on the ways in which you have been seeking comfort and security in material possessions. Identify one possession you can let go of and donate it to someone in need.

🫖PEARLS OF WISDOM 🫖

Coastal Lagoon (John 4:14): **
  - *Did you know? * Coastal lagoons are breeding grounds for diverse marine life.
  - *Parallel: * Jesus offering eternal life, like a coastal lagoon, is a source of new beginnings and spiritual rebirth.

✅Day 21: "Wellspring of Hope"

(Psalms 63:1)

Day 21 focuses on the metaphor of a wishing well and encourages us to continue our journey of thirsting for God, always hopeful and seeking His presence.

The key verse is Psalm 63:1, which says, "You, God, are my God, earnestly I seek you; I thirst for you, my whole being longs for you, in a dry and parched land where there is no water."

In this verse, the psalmist expresses a deep longing and thirst for God. The metaphor of a wishing well represents the ongoing journey of thirsting for God, always hopeful and seeking His presence.

A wishing well is a well or spring that is believed to have the power to grant wishes. It is a place where people come with hopes and desires, seeking something beyond themselves. Similarly, our journey of thirsting for God is a continuous pursuit of His presence and a longing for something greater than ourselves.

Thirsting for God is an expression of our deep need for Him. It is a recognition that our souls are restless until they find rest in Him. Just as a person in a dry and parched land longs for water to quench their thirst, our whole being longs for God and His presence to satisfy the deepest longings of our hearts.

The journey of thirsting for God is not a one-time event but a lifelong pursuit. It is a journey of seeking Him in prayer, studying His Word, and cultivating a relationship with Him. It is a journey of continually turning our hearts towards Him, always hopeful and expectant of His presence and guidance in our lives.

As we continue our journey of thirsting for God, we can find comfort and encouragement in knowing that He is always near. He is the source of living water that quenches our spiritual thirst and satisfies our deepest longings. He is the One who grants our wishes, not in the sense of material possessions, but in the sense of fulfilling the desires of our hearts according to His perfect will.

As we conclude this devotional journey we are encouraged to continue in our thirst for God, always hopeful and seeking His presence.

May we earnestly seek Him, longing for Him with our whole being. May we recognize that our souls find true rest and fulfillment in Him. May we continue to journey with Him, always hopeful and expectant of His presence and guidance in our lives.

❧ A **Deeper Dive…. ❧**

Celebrate the journey of quenching your spiritual thirst and the transformation you have experienced. Take a moment to thank God for His faithfulness and commit to continuing to seek Him above all.

🍪PEARLS OF WISDOM 🍪

Wishing Well (Psalms 63:1): **
- – *Did you know? * Wishing wells have roots in folklore, believed to grant wishes when coins are tossed.
- – *Parallel: * Our hopeful journey and thirst for God, like a wishing well, symbolize the belief in positive outcomes and divine blessings.

🙏🙏🙏

"Dear Heavenly Father,

We come before you today with hearts overflowing with gratitude and praise. We thank you for the 21-day journey we embarked upon, seeking to quench our spiritual thirst and find refreshment in your presence.

Just as water sustains and nourishes our physical bodies, you have provided us with the living water of your Word and the Holy Spirit to quench our spiritual thirst. We are grateful for the lessons we have learned, the insights we have gained, and the transformation we have experienced through this devotional journey.

Lord, you are the source of all living water. You are the well that never runs dry, the river that brings life to our souls. We thank you for your faithfulness in quenching our thirst, for meeting us in our times of need, and for guiding us along the path of righteousness.

As we conclude this devotional book, we pray for continued growth and deepening of our relationship with you. May the lessons we have learned and the truths we have discovered continue to shape and mold us into vessels of your love and grace.

We also pray for those who will come across this book in the future. May they too experience the refreshing and life-giving power of your living water. May they be drawn to you, their souls thirsting for the truth and satisfaction that can only be found in you.

Lord, we ask for your continued guidance and strength as we journey through life. Help us to remain rooted in your Word, to drink deeply from the well of your presence, and to share the water of life with those around us.

In Jesus' name, we pray. Amen." 🙏🙏🙏

"The Spirit and the bride say, 'Come!' And let him who hears say, 'Come!' Let him who is thirsty come, and let

everyone who wishes take the free gift of the water of life."
(Revelation 22:17)